MONSTERS
OF THE OLD SOUTH

JOHN LEMAY

BICEP BOOKS
ROSWELL, NEW MEXICO

An *Original* Publication of BICEP BOOKS

Copyright © 2020 by Bicep Books

All rights reserved. No portion of this book may be reproduced in any form without permission from the publisher, except as permitted by U.S. copyright law.

First Bicep Books printing August 2020

Printed in the USA

For Haley Jaconetti, one of the coolest ten-year-olds out there.

CONTENTS

Introduction...7

Chapter 1
The Alligator Man...9

Chapter 2
The White River Monster in the Civil War...19

Chapter 3
The Crocodingo...29

Chapter 4
Bigfoot Swims the Mississippi...35

Chapter 5
The Sharpshooter and the Swamp Monster...39

Chapter 6
The Legend of Green Eyes...45

Chapter 7
The Averasboro Gallinipper...51

Chapter 8
Virginia Snake Woman...55

Chapter 9
Devil Frog Monster of Indian Camp Spring...57

Chapter 10
The Bigfoot War of 1869...63
Chapter 11
The Monster of Osage Valley...67
Chapter 12
Southern Centaur...73
Chapter 13
The Kentucky Werewolf...77
Chapter 14
The Florida Mermaid...83
Chapter 15
Growl of the Gowrow...85
Chapter 16
Attack of the Giant Leeches...95
Chapter 17
Monster of the Mud Volcano...101
Chapter 18
The Mississippi Monster...111
Chapter 19
The Tennessee Lizard Man...117

About the Author...121

INTRODUCTION

When you first saw this book, you might have thought that it was fiction, but it's not. This is a book about what many people believe could be real monsters—creatures like Bigfoot, the Chupacabra, and the Loch Ness Monster.

Though some might scoff at the existence of such creatures, there are serious scientists and researchers who investigate the possibility that they are real. These people are called cryptozoologists. They consider creatures like Bigfoot and Chupacabras to simply be animals that haven't been officially discovered yet. Or, that is to say, even though hundreds of people claim to see these mysterious creatures every year, there's still no proof that they are actually real. These mystery animals are called cryptids.

Places all over the world have cryptids, they're just usually not as well-known as Scotland's Loch Ness

Monster, or Bigfoot, which is common to many forests the world over.

In this book's case, we're going to focus on monsters from a specific time period in a specific place: the Old South. The Old South refers to the Southern states of North America during the Pioneer Period, which roughly lasted from the early 1800s up until about 1915.

We will examine these mystery animals via actual accounts and newspaper articles from the time in many cases. Newspapers of the 1800s often reported on monster sightings. The only problem is that some of these articles were jokes. Making matters even worse, the newspapers never printed follow-up articles explaining whether or not the story was true, or was a reporter's prank.

But, as you read the book, you can decide for yourself whether these articles were simply a bored reporter's joke on readers, or if maybe, just maybe, they were describing real monsters...

CHAPTER 1
THE ALLIGATOR MAN

Even though most of the stories in this book take place over one hundred years ago, we are going to begin our next story in the summer of 1988. Late one night, seventeen-year-old Christopher Davis was driving along a lonely road near the Scape Ore Swamp of South Carolina. Just like a scene in a horror movie, he got a flat tire and had to pull over. Davis braved the spooky night air to change his tire. As soon as he was finished, he began to hear heavy footsteps behind him. He turned to look behind him and saw a seven-foot-tall monster with red, glowing eyes.

Davis jumped into his car and locked the door. The creature grabbed the door handle, but couldn't get inside.

As the monster hovered around his car, Davis could only see the beast from the neck down. He said that it had three big fingers ending in long blacks nails. The skin was rough and green. Davis started the car and began to drive away, but the thing began following him. When he looked in his rearview mirror, he could see the monster running behind him.

"I could see his toes and then he jumped on the roof of my car. I thought I heard a grunt and then I could see his fingers through the front windshield, where they curled around on the roof," Davis later told the police.

Davis sped up and began swerving the car, hoping to shake the monster off the roof of the car. When Davis slammed on his brakes, the monster was flung from the roof of the car onto the ground. Finally, Davis was able to escape the strange monster, which could only be described as a Lizard Man.

Scape Ore Swamp,
U.S. Geological Survey.

Witness Christopher Davis.

Davis told his story to the police. He also showed them his car, which had a damaged side-view mirror. Stranger yet, the roof of the car had claw marks on it. While this may not prove Davis's story, it did at least offer physical evidence to support his story. Davis even took a lie detector test and passed.

The young man soon became a celebrity of sorts and was even invited to appear on *The Oprah Winfrey Show*. Several other witnesses to the Lizard Man came forward. Two other men claimed to have seen the same creature two weeks before. Before that, a sighting was also recorded in 1987 by George Holliman Jr.

However, many skeptics still doubted that the Lizard Man existed. Many pointed to the fact that Davis changed his story in small ways during interviews. Others wanted to see photographic evidence of Davis's damaged car. Some even felt his lie detector test was faked.

But, what most of those skeptics didn't know was that a similar creature was seen in South Carolina nearly 100 years ago.

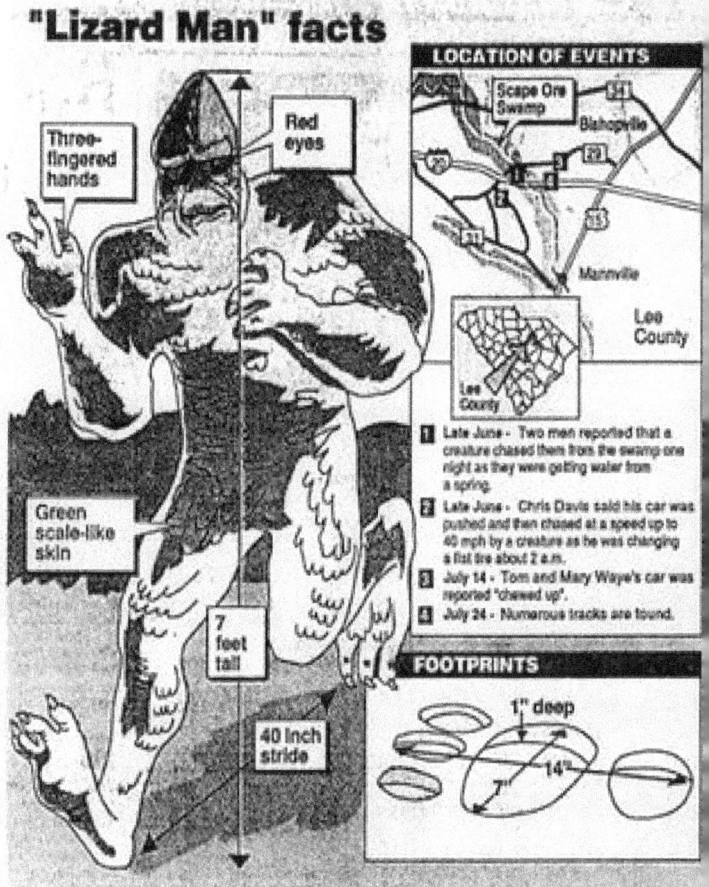

From the *Columbia State*,
August 15, 1988

One hundred sixty-four miles south of Scape Ore Swamp is Palmetto, South Carolina. On August 10, 1892, a newspaper called the *Woodland Daily Democrat* ran a story about a monster similar to Davis's Lizard Man. Only, the paper called their monster the "Alligator Man" instead. Other than the different names, the two creatures had a very similar description.

The newspaper story began by reporting how people living along Palmetto creek were "highly excited over the appearance of a strange and uncouth creature in that vicinity." The story said that the animal was seen in the waters of the creek, and also on land. This would seem to mean that the animal was an amphibian, like a frog.

The witnesses described it as looking like a cross between an ape and a reptile. While its skin was scaly like an alligator's, its stance and features were like that of a man or an ape's. Like a man, it had two arms and two legs, and it stood nine feet tall!

From the neck down, with the exception of some fin-shaped flippers, which extend from the arms to the waist, the creature resembles a man, only that the toes and fingers are armed with claws from two to six inches long," the paper reported.

The creature also had a forked tail like a fish would have. The witnesses, who saw the monster from a distance, said they thought the tail was probably about three feet long.

The monster left behind physical evidence in the form of tracks left in the mud. They were found around a place called Hennis Lake. The tracks were dug up and put on display in a drugstore in Donners Grove. Witnesses said the footprints measured over one foot long at 15 inches.

This was the last that was reported on the Alligator Man that we know of. It sounded quite similar to the Lizard Man of the 1980s. The main differences were that the Alligator Man was bigger at nine feet tall; the Lizard Man was seven feet. Also, the Lizard Man didn't have any fins like the Alligator Man did. The two creatures did have the same sized feet, though. Tracks of the Lizard Man were also found in 1988 and measured 14 inches (remember, the Alligator Man's tracks measured 15 inches).

Some might also ask, could the Alligator Man story from long ago have inspired the Lizard Man story? That's a good question, but the answer is no. The Alligator Man story was largely forgotten. Also, nobody brought up the 1892 Alligator Man when the Lizard Man was being discussed. So it does sound as though the witnesses back in 1892 and 1988 saw a similar creature in the same state.

Stranger still, creatures similar to the Lizard Man of South Carolina are seen all over the world. Ohio, West Virginia, Kentucky, New Jersey, and even Canada have had sightings reported of similar creatures. Then there's the Intulo of South Africa, the Cherufe Lizard Man of South America, the Nagas of India, and the mythical Kappas of Japan.

There are several theories for what these lizard-men could be, including an alien race known as the Reptilians. Also called reptoids, lizard people, and Draconians, the aliens have the form of a human being, but are covered in scales and have claws, sharp teeth, and sometimes, tails. Both of the creatures sighted in South Carolina could certainly pass for Reptilians.

Still, others believe that the Lizard Man could just be a heretofore unknown species of human-like dinosaur that survived into the modern era.

Whether it's an alien or a dinosaur, one thing's for sure: If you see it, run!

CHAPTER 2
THE WHITE RIVER MONSTER IN THE CIVIL WAR

"Welcome to Jacksonport, Home of the White River Monster" a sign proudly proclaims in the small Arkansas town located along the White River. Just like the town of Roswell, New Mexico, celebrates aliens and UFOs, Jacksonport is proud to call itself home to a monster. So proud, they even have an official refuge for the creature called the "White River Monster Refuge." The refuge was set up in February of 1973 by Senator Robert Harvey, who made it against the law to harm the monster, whether it's real or not.

However, it wasn't always this way. Back in the 1930s a few people tried to kill the monster. During this time four men signed an affidavit swearing they had seen the monster. One of the men, a farmer named Bramblett Bateman, said that on July 1, 1937, at one o'clock, he saw an object about 12 feet long and four to five-foot wide break the surface of the river. He also claimed to have seen it months later in September in the same location. Several of the workers on Batemen's farm had told him about the monster before his own sighting. The men said they had seen the beast, and they blamed it for the river's poor fishing that time of year.

After his sighting, Bateman called the sheriff's office to request a high powered rifle to kill the monster with. The sheriff's office obliged and sent several law officers to the river. One of them, Z.B. Reid, would later make his own sworn affidavit concerning the monster. According to Reid, he and several other men watched the river for several hours. When they were finally ready to go home, the monster showed. Reid caught a glimpse of it and said it reminded him of a giant sturgeon or catfish.

For many years the monster stayed hidden. Then, in the 1970s, it resurfaced and someone even took a photo of it. The photograph was captured back in the summer of 1971 by Cloyce Warren, who was fishing with some friends. The monster surfaced and Warren luckily had a camera. The photograph backs up many claims that the beast has a bony ridge along its back. Witnesses also describe the monster as having a bonelike protrusion coming from its forehead, though you can't see it in the photograph.

More evidence was found in the form of some tracks left behind by the monster on Towhead Island. They measured fourteen inches long and eight inches wide. Plaster casts were even made by the police department. The tracks were three-toed with claws. More were found later, along with flattened trees and grass.

The White River Monster photo from 1972 by Cloyce Warren.

The Towhead Island tracks inspired a local trapper, Ollie Ritcherson, and a 13-year-old boy, Joey Dupree, to take a boat out to the island. Although they didn't see the monster, their boat hit an object moving through the water. Though they couldn't see it, they believe that it was the monster, and for a moment the boat was lifted onto the creature's back for a few brief moments.

After that there would be only one more sighting of the monster that year by a man named Jim Gates. He watched the monster thrash around in the water for a full 15 minutes. In 1972 a vacationing family saw the monster near Jacksonport Park and estimated it to be nearly 60 to 75 feet long! That is much bigger than previous sightings where witnesses estimated the beast to be around 20 feet long at the most. R.C. McClauglen, the father of the group, said he could see some sort of head and a spiny backbone just like the other witnesses.

Old picture of an Elephant Seal.

MONSTERS OF THE OLD SOUTH

After an extensive investigation of the sightings, cryptozoologist Dr. Roy P. Mackal came to the conclusion that the White River Monster was likely an elephant seal. His reasoning for this was that one had likely gotten into the Mississippi River and then trailed off into the White River. Also, witnesses' descriptions described behavior much similar to an elephant seal, such as the loud bellowing noises heard as well as its surfacing patterns and skin texture/color. The boney protrusion described by Ernest Denks could be attributed to an elephant seal's protruding nose and "trunk."

However, some witnesses described the monster as serpent-like. Also, the grainy photograph by Cloyce Warren appears to show a spiny back of some sort, leading one to wonder how an elephant seal could have such an appearance. Then there are the witnesses from 1972 who claimed the monster they saw was over 60 feet long, which is much larger than any elephant seal could ever get.

Example of Civil War-era gunboat.

But, whatever the White River Monster is or isn't, it might just be a war veteran. You see, accounts of the monster went back much further than the 1930s. A woman from Little Rock claimed to have seen it in 1915. There are even some Native American legends that seem to refer to the monster. But, most interesting of all, folklore claims that the monster took part in the Civil War. Specifically, it was rumored that the monster was responsible for overturning a Confederate gunboat in Arkansas White River. Further stories say that it overturned other boats in the river, and yet another story had soldiers shooting at it from the riverbanks.

However, even though there is substantial evidence to support the White River Monster's existence, even the monster's supporters admit there's a possibility the Civil War stories were created after the creature became popular. So bottom line, yes, there probably is a White River Monster of some kind, but its participation in the Civil War is uncertain. But it's definitely a cool story!

The Crocodingo.

CHAPTER 3
THE CROCODINGO

The animal we are about to discuss in this chapter is definitely one of the weirdest monsters ever covered in cryptozoology. It is called the Crocodingo, and is essentially a dingo with the head of a crocodile. If you think that's weird, just wait until you hear its origin story.

On the night of July 31, 1839, a farmer named Hank Lemon had what could be considered an alien encounter in Huntsville, Tennessee. Lemon noticed a strange, green glow in the sky behind his home. Creepier still, his dogs seemed upset by the strange light. And then, "a dead straight bolt of lightning" hit the ground. The green glow dissipated, and moments later he saw a strange "horribly alien" looking creature dart from the woods. He described it as having the body of a dog with the head of a crocodile.

Lemon also reported on a horrible smell which he called a "horrible charnel stench in the air..." He also said that the smell "would drive a man crazy" if he were "exposed to it for too long..."

The strange animal was seen off and on from 1856 to 1860 near a place called New River, Tennessee. The creature was supposedly seen catching fish from a creek quite often. Some fishermen even left fish out for the animal as an offering of a sort. For a while, the creature was known as the Haint Dog. In the late 1800s, Curiel Allan Brown, whose father was an Australian immigrant, nicknamed the strange animal the "Crocodingo." (Dingos, you know, are native to Australia).

A notable encounter with the Crocodingo occurred during the Civil War. A Confederate soldier named

Roger Owens claimed that he saw the Crocodingo guarding a freshly killed soldier. Did the monster kill the man, or did he simply find the body? Owens did not know, but when he returned later, he found only blood. The body and the dog were gone.

Other Confederate soldiers reported seeing the beast, claiming that it watched them from a distance and sometimes growled at them. Sometimes they saw it running through the woods.

The sightings continued after the Civil War, too. In the early 1900s, fishermen began to notice that there weren't as many fish in New River and they blamed it on the Crocodingo. Farmers shot at the animal and set traps for it, but they never were able to catch or harm the creature.

As time carried on, so did the Crocodingo. Railroad workers in the vicinity of Oneida, Tennessee, claimed to find freshly placed rails with bite marks on them. They thought that the Crocodingo must have done it.

Sightings reached a peak in the year 1925, after the completion of the

Oneida Sewer System. Locals began to report strange cries coming from the sewer drains. These awful "alien cries" could be heard after a heavy rain. The next day, manholes would be found overturned, suggesting that something crawled out of the sewers.

In 1943, a man named Jack Bannister claimed that he followed a strange animal that he thought was a coyote into the sewer. He said that it acted like a dog by nudging open the manhole and then "slithered down into the sewer." Bannister eventually got a good look at the animal, which he said had the body of a "mangy wolf" with the head of a crocodile. The next significant sighting would not occur until the next century, in 2012, when two witnesses saw the animal emerge from a sewer again.

But what is the Crocodingo? Because of the first sighting recorded by Hank Lemon in 1839, many people think the Crocodingo could be an alien animal of some sort. Specifically, they think the animal could be a genetically engineered cross between a crocodile and a dog! Again, the reason why people associate it with aliens is because Hank Lemon claimed he saw a green glow and lightning before the monster appeared.

But, if we were to consider the green glow and the lightning to be a coincidence, then we could consider other explanations for the Crocodingo. The animal could be a prehistoric survivor from the days of the dinosaurs. Believe it or not, there were hair-covered prehistoric reptiles that looked similar to dogs. They were called the Cynognathus and belonged to the Therapsid family. The book *Dinosaurs and Other Prehistoric Animals* even writes that they "looked like a cross between a wolf and a lizard" on page 72.

If a person from the 1800s saw a hairy reptile on all fours, they might describe it as a dog with the head of a crocodile. So, perhaps what they were really seeing was a therapsid of some sort all along?

Therapsids as drawn by classic artist Charles Knight.

CHAPTER 4
BIGFOOT SWIMS THE MISSISSIPPI

One of the most famous cryptids known to man is Bigfoot. The tall, ape-like creature is seen all over the world and goes under different names depending on where it's seen. Canadians call it Sasquatch, Russians call it the Alma, and in Tibet the creature is called the Yeti or Abominable Snowman. In the South, due to its horrible smell, it is often called the "Skunk Ape."

The following story presents a unique Bigfoot encounter in that the witnesses saw the creature swimming, something that doesn't happen often in Bigfoot accounts.

The sighting took place near Vicksburg, Mississippi, in September of 1867. A party of hunters was riding through the swampland a few miles from the Mississippi River. Their hounds became excited by something and broke away from the hunters, following a scent that took them off the main trail.

The men rushed to follow their hounds and could see strange footprints in the mud. The footprints looked like those belonging to a human except that the "toes of one foot turned backward."

Finally, they caught up with the dogs, which were barking at a "frightful-looking creature." They said that it had the appearance and height of a man, except that it was much more muscular and covered in body hair three inches long. The men also claimed that the hair on the man-thing's head was so long that it reached its knees.

Different from many other Bigfoot sightings, it also had tusks, or large front teeth that were several inches long.

Alleged photo of Bigfoot taken in the 1970s.

As the hunters approached it, the beast ran towards the Mississippi River. The men and dogs cornered the creature for a second time at the river's edge, but everyone was too afraid to go near it. The man-thing was also afraid of the hunters, and so it dove into the river. The men said that it "quickly swam away disappearing from sight."

That was the end of their sighting, but on June 27, 1868, the *St. Louis Dispatch* received a letter from a man in the village of Meadville, Mississippi. He reported that a "strange creature" had been "causing much excitement in that usually monotonous village." The man said that people were "agitated on account of the strange creature seen near here." The letter also stated that the creature looked similar to an animal seen near Vicksburg the previous fall.

So, does Vicksburg have its own variety of Bigfoot? The answer is most likely yes, and similar creatures are still seen there to this day. As recently as 2014, Bigfoot tracks were found in a playground in Vicksburg...

CHAPTER 5
THE SHARPSHOOTER AND THE SWAMP MONSTER

G.B. Shaw served as the sheriff of the Vermilion Parish of New Orleans, Louisiana, from 1868 to 1872. He was also a nationally ranked marksman and sharpshooter. According to a story in the *Burlington Hawk Eye* on June 27, 1883, Shaw also saw a swamp monster.

The sighting took place in the swamplands of Lake Catherine. With Shaw at the time were two other men, one of whom was the keeper of the Lake Catherine club. The three men were out hunting when "their attention was attracted by a great disturbance in the waters of the bayou."

G.B. Shaw.

The paper reported that the men rushed to the bank of the stream where they saw "a reptile, whose immensity and revolting ugliness amazed them beyond measure." The monster's body was protruding from the reeds, and they estimated it to be thirty feet long and three feet wide. They claimed that the creature had a back topped with horns that they thought were six to ten inches long. The monster's tail was under the water, but the men could tell the monster was propelling itself with a tail through the water. "As the monster moved great waves were raised and broke among the reeds," the paper reported.

As to the animal's head, they compared it to an alligator. The men shot at the monster with buckshot. "The monster reared its huge, repulsive head full six feet above the water, and its red, glittering eyes glared fiercely toward its enemies," the paper wrote. The men "were almost paralyzed with the horror of the dreadful apparition" but still managed to fire a second round of shots at the creature. The monster roared and revealed a big mouth with a "cavernous throat, from which flashed a long slender tongue."

The monster swam away and disappeared into a huge section of reeds within the swamp. "As it disappeared the gentlemen were still further terrified with a muffled roar," the paper reported. The men fired into the reeds in hopes that the monster would reappear, but it was never seen again.

Even though newspapers back then loved to make up stories like these, I think there's a chance this one is true. I think this because if you were to make up a story with a famous marksman like G.B. Shaw, why not end the story with him shooting it between the eyes and killing it? Lots of fake newspaper stories existed where a monster of some sort was killed. The article would often boldly claim that the body would be shipped off to the Smithsonian Institute. But, of course, they never were. G.B. Shaw's story is almost boring by comparison in that he simply shoots at the monster and it gets away.

MONSTERS OF THE OLD SOUTH

The prehistoric Desmatosuchus.

Also, the monster described in the story matches very well with a known dinosaur called the Desmatosuchus. The animal looked like a crocodile with a spiky back, which is exactly what the witnesses in the story described seeing. In fact, the name Desmatosuchus means "link crocodile." Despite its scary appearance, it was a plant-eater, and the spikes on its back were likely to protect it from carnivores.

Due to the fact that the creature in this story matches well with a known dinosaur, and also because the story is not terribly fantastic, all things considered, I think there's a good chance that it just might be true.

CHAPTER 6
THE LEGEND OF GREEN EYES

The Battle of Chickamauga was one of the bloodiest battles in the Civil War. It is ranked by many as second only to the Battle of Gettysburg in terms of how many people died. The Battle of Chickamauga raged for two days (September 19-20) in 1863 in southeastern Tennessee and northwestern Georgia.

Legend has it that the battle was preceded by a bad omen. The night before the fight began, two Tennessee soldiers supposedly heard an unearthly shriek come from the woods. The soldiers crept to the edge of the woods and saw a hairy, ten-foot-tall monster. Its eyes glowed like hot coals, and it smelt like rotten meat. When the soldiers ran back to camp to tell their commander of the monster they saw, no one believed them. The next morning, a sergeant went to the spot where they saw the creature and found 22-inch footprints in the earth. The creature sounds an awful lot like Bigfoot.

But, Bigfoot wasn't the only strange creature associated with the battle. A strange being today called "Green Eyes" was also glimpsed. The human-like creature was seen after the battle was over, and witnesses claimed that it was eating the bodies of the dead! It was humanoid in form, but with great jaws full of fanged teeth. It was said to be short and had long straw-like hair flowing from its head. It also had glowing green eyes that struck terror into those who saw it.

Some legends later claimed that it was the ghost of a soldier killed during the battle. What's more, it's still seen at the sight of the Battle of Chickamauga to this day.

MONSTERS OF THE OLD SOUTH

The Battle of Chickamauga.

There have been a few stories about the drivers of cars seeing the intense, glowing green eyes when they drive near the battlefield. A few times, the eyes were so intense that they caused the driver to have an accident. Two accidents that people know of occurred in the 1970s.

During the year 1976, a park ranger named Edward Tinney said that he was walking through the park at four o'clock in the morning when he saw Green Eyes. He said that before he saw it, a chill ran through his body. And then he saw it. A green-eyed being stepped from the shadows and into his view.

"When it passed me, I could see his hair was long like a woman's," Tinney said. "The eyes – I'll never forget those eyes – they were glaring, almost greenish-orange in color, flashing like some sort of wild animal. The teeth were long and pointed like fangs."

The monster mysteriously disappeared when the headlights of a car driving by shown on it. So, if you like to tour old battlegrounds of the Civil War, beware of Chickamauga...

MONSTERS OF THE OLD SOUTH

Green Eyes by Neil Riebe.

Depiction of a giant mosquito that appeared in *The Strand Magazine* in 1909.

CHAPTER 7
THE AVERASBORO GALLINIPPER

On the banks of the Cape Fear River once sat the wild town of Averasboro. The town was wild due to visits from rowdy woodsmen who worked at cutting timber near the river. In one of the Averasboro bars hung the "skeleton" of a monster mosquito.

I put quotation marks around the word skeleton because insects don't have skeletons. Insects have their skeletons on the outside rather than the inside and are called exoskeletons.

What was hanging up in the bar was just a model of the monster called the Averasboro Gallinipper. People figured it was probably just the skeleton of a large bird that had something resembling a needle placed where the beak used to be.

Though the skeleton was definitely fake, could it have been based on a real monster? There's a small chance that it was, because local Native American myths spoke of just such a creature. The Tuscarora tribe of North Carolina claimed that the state was the birthplace of the mosquito. The first mosquito, they said, was a giant called Ro-tay-yo that came from underneath the grounds of the Neuse River.

This mosquito was said to be as big as a full-grown man. The Tuscarora chief, Elias Johnson, wrote that the creature made a loud noise when it flew. With its long stinger, it would completely drain the blood of the people it landed on. Johnson claimed that many Tuscarora warriors died fighting the monster and that none could kill it.

Eventually, the monster flew north, to Onondaga in present-day New York State. A warrior named Tarenyawagon chased the creature all the way to the

Great Lakes and killed it with an arrow. From its blood were born the smaller mosquitos we know today.

It's unknown if workmen in 1850's Averasboro heard the Tuscarora legends or if they simply made up tales of their own. Whatever the case, they claimed that the swamps were infested by mosquitos as large as birds!

Some of the men seemed to truly believe in these oversized bugs, while others just enjoyed telling tall tales about them. One of the more famous stories about the creatures was dug up by historian Malcolm Fowler. The story went that in 1855 two groups of workmen were cutting timber deep in the forest along Beaverdam Swamp. One group was from Chatham County and the others were from the town of Averasboro. The Chatham County men bet that Red Saunders, the toughest man in their group, could lie facedown shirtless for one hour and endure the mosquitos without flinching.

According to the legend, Saunders lasted fifty-five minutes before the Gallinipper came along. Red Billy

Avera saw it first and cried out, "What is that!?" Though Avera pointed to the sky, no one could see any monster mosquitos. But then Saunders cried out in pain—as if bitten by a giant mosquito.

Saunders lost his bet, though it's likely the Gallinipper wasn't to blame. Supposedly someone threw a hot cole on his back!

While the giant mosquitos spoken of by the timber workers are most certainly mythical, one still has to wonder about those from Native American legend...

CHAPTER 8
VIRGINIA SNAKE WOMAN

Just as there was supposedly an Alligator Man in South Carolina, Virginia once had reports of a "Snake Woman." If an article published in an old newspaper on September 19, 1907, is to be believed, there really was a "Half Woman and Snake" crawling through the countryside!

The article claimed that an expedition had set out from Jamestown, Virginia, to see for themselves whether or not the supposed Snake Woman was real.

According to the stories, the woman's skin was scaly like a snake's. Not only that, she was said to crawl across the ground on all fours looking for mice and other small animals to devour. When she ate them, she would swallow them whole just like a snake the stories said. Even grosser, she was said to shed her skin once a year just like a snake!

For years people thought she was a tall tale until a mountain man named Stone Colby claimed to see her with his own eyes. It was Colby who excited the Jamestown men into going on an expedition to capture her.

There were never any follow-up stories to the one published in 1907. Nor are there any Snake Women seen in Virginia today. So, perhaps she was the last of her kind? Or, maybe she was just a tall tale after all...

CHAPTER 9
DEVIL FROG MONSTER OF INDIAN CAMP SPRING

I'm skeptical of the story we are about to discuss not because it's about a giant frog, but because stories about frogs were popular around this time.

In 1865, Mark Twain published his famous story, "The Celebrated Jumping Frog of Calaveras County." In the story, two men bet on whose frog can jump the farthest. While one man has his back turned, the other makes his frog swallow lead. That way the frog will be weighed down and can't jump as far. The comedic story went on to make Mark Twain famous and is well remembered to this day.

The story we are about to discuss is not so well remembered. It came out in 1869, four years after Twain's famous story. It was published in the *Nashville Union and American* on March 14, 1869, and told of a giant frog weighing 93 pounds!

The story concerns a Mr. Lem. Matthews, who wrote to the paper to tell them the fantastic story. Mr. Matthews claimed that his two sons (one was eleven and the other thirteen) had discovered a cave near their house. Within the cave they found "a monster frog, as large as a hogshead."

Though he thought his two boys were either exaggerating or pulling a good-natured joke on him, he decided to return to the cave with them. As backup, he also brought along six neighbors.

The group of men and boys ventured into the cave with torches and candles. Eventually, they found the monstrous frog. Matthews claimed it wasn't as big as his boys had claimed, but that it was still the biggest frog he had ever seen. It was so big that the men were afraid to get within twenty feet of it.

1800s era illustration of frog.

Matthews called the frog a "hideous sight!" He wrote that "Its eyes, as they glistened in the torch light, made such an impression upon me, and in fact upon the whole party, that we trembled as if in the presence of a real demon, for in all my imaginations of the appearance of a demon, I must acknowledge that I never conceived of anything that would be calculated to fill the mind with such a horror as this."

One of the men tossed a stone at the giant frog. The frog monster then leaped ten feet across the cave in their direction. The men darted away from the creature. Once there was a safe distance between them, they began making plans to capture the beast.

One of the men went back to his house and secured a large box, or crate, to catch the frog. Once the box arrived at the cave, the men tossed stones at the frog until it was cornered against the cave wall. The men then placed the open crate above the frog and trapped it inside. Tipping it over, they then placed a sheet of wood over the bottom and nailed it down, trapping the poor frog inside.

The men claimed that it took great effort to drag the crate out of the cave. The men weighed the frog back at a neighbor's house and determined it to be 93 pounds! They also measured the animal and said that it was over three feet tall when in a sitting position. They then set the frog loose in a chicken coop. Nobody knows what happened to the frog after that, if it even existed at all. But, what if it did?

The largest frog in existence today is the African Goliath Frog, which can grow as big as a rabbit. As its name suggests, it is native to Africa, so finding one in the U.S. would have been a stretch.

But, there is another contender for the frog monster. During the days of the dinosaurs lived a monster frog called *Beelzebufo ampinga* ("lord of the flies") by today's scientists. This giant frog was still nowhere near as big as the one described in the newspaper article. It was only a little larger than the African Goliath Frog and is thought to have weighed ten pounds at most.

Considering that the animal lived during the late Cretaceous, it is thought that the frog could have devoured small dinosaurs due to its larger than normal mouth! The first fossil remains were discovered by David W. Krause in 1993.

In summary, though the African Goliath Frog and the prehistoric *Beelzebufo ampinga* could explain the creature in the story, more likely than not, it was just a tall tale made up for people's amusement.

CHAPTER 10
THE BIGFOOT WAR OF 1869

For true believers in the existence of Bigfoot, it comes as no surprise that many Native American tribes talked of hairy giants who lived in the woods. They did not call them Bigfoot, as that name would be invented much later.

The following story was published in the *Dunkirk Observer Journal* on July 16, 1889. However, that is not when the story takes place. The article retells an older tale from years before.

The story tells of a small, unnamed Native American tribe that lived in the area of what is now Oconee County, South Carolina. The tribe was briefly terrorized by a being described as being "seven feet high" and "covered with hair."

When the tribe left their camp along the Tugalo River to go hunting, they left behind a deer they had killed the day before. When they returned that night, the deer was gone. The same thing happened again the next day. On the third day, one of the members of the tribe stayed behind to watch.

To his amazement, the man watched as a hairy giant walked into the camp and picked up another deer carcass. The man was too afraid to fight the beast, which he said also had sharp claws.

The next day, all seven members of the hunting party stayed at camp. Just as the man said, the monster came again and scooped up another fresh kill. One of the men aimed a rifle at the monster as it walked away and shot it in the back. The beast turned around to face his attacker and began walking towards him. All the other men fired their guns into the monster, and it fell dead.

Still image taken from footage captured of Bigfoot in 1967.

But that isn't the end of the story. Three hours later, the men heard a fearsome yell. It sounded like someone yelling, "Yahoo, yahoo, yahoo!"

The men left camp and called on a Sheriff from a nearby town for assistance. The sheriff and his men came to the hunting party's aid. The sheriff also brought hunting dogs to search out the source of the noise.

The dogs led the men to a monster just like the one that had been killed earlier. The creature drove away the dogs whenever they attacked. Eventually, the men chased it to a river. It swam to the other side, and the article says that a little bit later, another hunting party shot and killed the monster.

And what happened to the body? Sadly, nobody knows...

CHAPTER 11
THE MONSTER OF OSAGE VALLEY

One day back in the spring of 1844 in St. Clair County, Missouri, a farmer named Matthew Arbuckle was plowing his field. Suddenly, Arbuckle heard a monstrous roar come from the river, located one mile from his farm.

Terrified, Arbuckle saddled his horse and rode it to the nearest town: Papinville, about fifteen miles away. The townspeople were shocked to see how Arbuckle was pale with fear, and the horse was exhausted from the frantic pace Arbuckle rode it at.

Steamboat along the Osage River.

With shallow breaths, Arbuckle told the people of Papinville how he had barely escaped from an awful monster. "He had not seen the fearful beast, he confessed, but he had heard its voice, by which he knew it to be a monster of terrific proportions," said a newspaper article detailing the story.

Arbuckle's report of the monster convinced his neighbors to take up a hunt for the beast to stop it from harming anyone. A group of armed men gathered the next morning to hunt the creature. Before they had set out, one of their daughters, a girl named Mattie, had gone down to the river to fetch water.

Suddenly, the men all heard the terrifying roar that Arbuckle had heard the day before. The father of the girl down at the river, named Mr. Whitley, feared for his daughter's life.

"Charge, men!" roared Whitley, grabbing his gun. "Mattie went to the river for water, and I reckon she's dead afore now!"

The crowd rushed towards the river, determined to rescue the girl. They encountered Mattie on the way to the river. And though the girl was also frightened by the roar of the monster, she hadn't seen it.

The hunters marched on towards the river, hearing the strange noise of the monster from time to time. The men were frustrated because their hound dogs could pick up no scent to track. The men searched all day long until a storm broke out, and so they had to take shelter in a cave.

The men were awakened the next morning by the monster's roar yet again. They grabbed their guns and set out for the river as the roar became louder and louder...

As they neared closer, they could hear the beast puffing and snorting as it swam through the water. When the men arrived at the riverbank, each hid behind a tree with their guns ready as they waited for the monster to swim past them.

A moment later, the monster came around the bend. It was a large steamboat named the *Flora Jones!* On the boat's deck was a happy crowd of passengers watching the sun rise. The men stepped from behind the trees, their mouths open in shock, as the friendly passengers waved to them as they passed by. The steamboat let out a loud whistle. It was the same as the monster's roar.

You see, the *Flora Jones* was the first steamboat to travel up the Osage River. None of the people there had ever heard the loud whistle of a steamboat, and so they had thought it was the roar of a monster.

This actual humorous event was reported years later in the July 10, 1907 edition of the *Clarke Courier*. If you are like me, you are probably disappointed that this story didn't feature a real monster.

However, this story still proves one thing: people back then really did believe in monsters...

The mythical centaur named Chiron teaching Achilles how to play the lyre.

CHAPTER 12
SOUTHERN CENTAUR

In Greek mythology, the centaur was a half-man half-horse. Specifically, it had the upper body of a man attached to the lower body of a horse. I'm not sure that the writers of the article we're about to cover knew what a Greek centaur really was. Though it doesn't fit the description of the mythical animal exactly, they chose to call the strange mammal seen in Arkansas in 1877 a "Mexican Centaur" (apparently they thought the animal was native to Mexico for some reason).

The article was published in *The Arkansas Journal* on June 30, 1877. The article began, "Dr. Collins of Little River County killed a most remarkable quadruped near his place in the spring of 1877." Quadruped, by the way, means an animal that walks on all fours like a dog or a horse.

The article goes on that the strange animal was first seen during the Civil War (but doesn't give any interesting details). The article said that people described the creature as a "large red deer, with the head and neck of a man."

Dr. Collin's wife and a young girl were walking along a path in the woods when they noticed the animal staring at them. They ran home and told the doctor what they had seen. He grabbed his gun and went out to look for the beast. When Dr. Collins saw the animal, he told the paper that the creature looked scared and began to cry! Dr. Collins shot the animal anyways, and it leaped into the air. As it lay dying, it let out a series of screams and yelps that sounded almost human.

But, when Dr. Collins looked at the dead animal, he found that its head wasn't really like that of a human's like so many had said. It looked more like the head of a baboon.

The article went on to say that the animal's eyes were placed on the sides of its head rather than in front. It had a long brown beard along its chin and neck.

The article ended by stating that, "It is generally believed that the creature was a species of Mexican centaur, a semi-legendary creature of the post-conquest era." Where the reporters got the idea that Centaurs were from Mexico rather than the mythology of Greece is unknown.

And, as usual, we don't know whether the article was made up for the amusement of readers, or if it really did happen.

Depiction of werewolf from 1493.

CHAPTER 13
THE KENTUCKY WEREWOLF

Back in the early 1800s, a man named Nils Wills was hunting in Red River Gorge, Kentucky, when he stumbled and fell from a high cliff. He was found near death by some friends from the Cherokee Native American tribe.

They brought him back to their camp and asked the tribal elders if they could help. The elders knew of only one method, something called the "Wolf Gift." The elders performed a strange ceremony on Wills, which completely healed him of his wounds. But like all fairy tales, this gift came with a terrible curse. From that day forward, Wills turned into a werewolf, which the Cherokee called the *Limikin*. Wills was mortified by the strange transformation that overtook him, and so he made it his mission in life to kill the tribal elders who had changed him into a wolf. After the elders were dead, he even hunted down their families!

According to legend, Wills killed any Cherokee person he came into contact with until his death in 1810. Or, presumed death, we should say. To this day, when hikers go missing—or half-eaten human remains are discovered—the Wills Werewolf is still blamed.

As recently as November of 2015 something similar to the Wills Werewolf was spotted in Red River Gorge by campers. The beast was never clearly seen, and the witness observed only two red eyes. The witness said that the monster made noises that sounded like a man being killed combined with a wolf's howl.

The Wills Werewolf wasn't the only monster of its kind in Kentucky, though. In an area called "The Land Between Lakes" there have been

MONSTERS OF THE OLD SOUTH

reports of a seven-foot-tall werewolf for many years. French traders spoke of a *loup-garou* (the French word for werewolf) in the area before the Louisiana Purchase of 1803.

There are two versions of the legend. One comes from European settlers, and the other comes from Native American tribes. The European legend goes that an immigrant family from Europe came to America in the early 1800s to settle in the land "Between the Rivers." The father of the group supposedly carried a genetic disease that he had also passed down to his children. This mysterious condition caused the family to "go mad" after nightfall. The family stayed away from other people, and the children never even went to school. Many years later, in the 1900s, their homestead was found abandoned. Strangely, no dead bodies were found, and where the family went is a mystery. But, some people today think that the family or their descendants are to blame for monster sightings in the area.

The Native American version of the legend goes that there was once a

Chickasaw shaman who could shapeshift into a wolf. He was accused by his fellow tribesmen of using his powers for evil and was cast out into the wilderness. But even that wasn't enough for the tribe. Some of the tribe felt the shaman should be killed. When not enough Chickasaw people agreed to help hunt down their old shaman, the angry tribesmen went to a saloon. There they asked rowdy cowboys for help in hunting down the wolf-man.

The group went out into the wild and shot the shaman in his wolf form. In his dying moments, the shaman cursed the men and vowed to return to torment them. And, sure enough, soon after strange howls came from the woods, hunters mysteriously disappeared, and bison were killed by a hideous predator. Stranger still, livestock were occasionally found dead but not eaten. This is unusual because animals typically only kill other animals to eat them. For this reason, it seemed as though the killings came out of spite.

Eventually, settlers caught a glimpse of the strange creature which resembled a wolf walking upright on two legs. Tales spread of families huddling within their cabins in fear as they listened to the creature walk across their porch. The next morning they would find deep gouges—claw marks—in the wood.

One man claimed that it jumped out of one of the horse stalls in front of him one night, causing him to wet his pants. Another old-timer and his wife claimed to see it get tangled in chicken wire while trying to get into their chicken coop. To this day, stories persist of the Kentucky werewolf. An urban legend even exists that claims a whole family of campers was killed by the monster in the 1980s. According to the legend, the story was covered up by local authorities...

CHAPTER 14
THE FLORIDA MERMAID

Though mermaids are simply thought to be the stuff of mythology, there are scholars who believe that most myths are based in truth. Furthermore, many people hundreds of years ago believed in mermaids. By the time the story we are about to cover was published in 1890, most people no longer believed in mermaids. Therefore, we have to ask ourselves, was the author of this article using the mythical mermaid as the basis for a made-up story, or did a fisherman back in 1890 really catch a genuine mermaid?

The story goes that on April 29, a man named W.W. Stanton was fishing off the coast of St. Augustine, Florida. He felt something heavy catch on his fishing line, and when he drew it up, he found the strangest creature he had ever seen.

It was six feet long and pure white. The article, published in the *Marion Daily Star* on May 13, 1890, said that "The head and face are wonderfully human in shape and feature. The shoulders are well outlined, and very much resemble those of a woman..." The article reported that the body looked human until it reached the waist, at which point in began to resemble a fish.

The paper wrote that it had four flippers below the waist. It was still alive when fished aboard, and made a strange human-like noise. The poor mermaid lived for two days after its capture and then died. The article concluded by stating that, "Mr. Stanton, after visiting several ports and showing his queer creature, will donate it to the Smithsonian Institution."

CHAPTER 15
GROWL OF THE GOWROW

Of all Arkansas' monsters, the best known is probably the Gowrow. The Gowrow is described as a 20-foot reptile with tusks and claws similar to an ankylosaurus. It was first reported on New Year's Eve of 1897 in an article called "The Green Gowrow, Killed in Searcy County."

The story told of a businessman named William Miller, who, while visiting a town called Blanco, heard reports of the monstrous Gowrow. According to the townspeople, the monster was eating everything it could sink its claws into: cattle, horses, hogs, dogs, and cats.

Newspapers claimed that this drawing of the Gowrow was based upon a photograph.

The monster had terrorized the town for several months. Attempts had been made to capture it, but all of them had failed. The monster would come down from the mountains at night to devour whatever it could find.

Miller asked the townspeople why they called it the Gowrow, and they said it was because that was what the "awful cry it uttered" sounded like,

Miller arrived after snow had fallen within the town. A young man out hunting rabbits stumbled upon the Gowrow's tracks in the snow. He told the townspeople of his discovery.

"We formed a posse, armed ourselves with shotguns and Winchesters and started in hot pursuit of the Gowrow," Miller wrote. "We followed the tracks without difficulty for several miles through the new fallen snow until they disappeared at the river bank."

The hunting party walked along the river until they discovered a huge cave, which they figured to be the creature's home. The men lit torches and fearfully crept inside. In the beast's lair they found "countless skeletons and skulls of all kinds and sizes, many of them evidently those of unfortunate human beings, while others seem to have belonged to horses, sheep, hogs, dogs and wild animals..." Miller reported.

The men left the cave and went outside so that they could hide and ambush the animal when it returned. After about thirty minutes, they could hear something making its way towards them in the water.

Miller said that the monster was green, and had two huge tusks jutting from under its lip. Its legs, he said, were short and thick. Its feet were webbed like a duck's, except that it had claws too. Along its back ran a series of sharp horns, which came to an abrupt end near the root of the tail. The tail was long and thin and ended with a sharp bone like a sickle.

Miller claims he took a snapshot of the monster with a Kodak camera. (For those wondering, yes, the Kodak camera had been invented by then). After getting a picture, he commanded the other men to fire their guns on the beast.

The numerous bullets were enough to mortally wound the monster. But, the Gowrow didn't die peacefully. It writhed and thrashed around in the forest, and the sharp bone at the end of its tail cut down several trees. Miller even claims that the monster cut off a man's leg with its tail!

After a while, the wild Gowrow finally quit moving and died. Miller speculated that the animal was something from prehistoric times, and vowed to send the remains to the Smithsonian in Washington.

But don't get too excited. If you were to ask the Smithsonian about the bones today, they probably wouldn't know what you were talking about. The Encyclopedia of Arkansas writes, "Williams claimed to have sent the body to the Smithsonian Institution, but it never arrived at the Washington DC museum." An article in the *Salina Journal* in 1951 wrote that "The Smithsonian denied receiving it and Miller always insisted that some minor official up there probably embezzled his trophy."

Drawing of the alleged second Gowrow photo.

The editor who published the original story, Fred W. Allsopp, even said, "It was a great fake, probably without foundation in fact." Furthermore, the photograph that Miller claimed to have snapped has never surfaced. And speaking of photographs, yet another man claimed to snap a picture of the monster not long after.

An article published on March 9, 1898, in the *Daily Arkansas Gazette* tells of a man's struggle against a baby Gowrow. The man was named C. B. Webb, and claimed that he was attacked by a "hideous looking animal about the size of a dog." Webb fought the beast with his ax and killed it. "A Ledger artist was nearby with a kodak and took a snap shot just as the gowrow was in the act of springing upon Cuthbert," the paper claimed.

For many years, this was the last we would hear of the Gowrow. Then in 1927 came a story about a group of people exploring a place called Diamond Cave.

FAIRY FENCING ROOM, DIAMOND CAVERNS, JASPER, ARK.

Deep within the cave, the party of explorers found a dark, mysterious hole. The strangest thing about the hole is that the tracks of a large animal led up to it and disappeared. To see how deep the hole went, they tossed a rope with an iron bar attached to it down the hole.

The party heard a frightening hiss, and when they pulled the rope back up, the iron looked like it had teeth marks in it! Next, they tossed a rope with a stone attached to it down the hole. There was another hiss, and this time the rope came back up bitten in two. They repeated their experiment several times until one of the party suggested that perhaps the hole was the home of the mighty Arkansas Gowrow.

The man was a reporter who just happened to have the old article written by William Miller with him. The reporter read the article to the astonished party and concluded that the old Gowrow must have faked his death and then made his way to Diamond Cave, where he has been in hiding ever since...

Giant leech from the Amazon.

CHAPTER 16
ATTACK OF THE GIANT LEECHES

We covered a giant mosquito earlier in this book, now prepare yourself for a similar legend about giant leeches. Just like the Averasboro Gallinipper, the giant leeches of Native American legend also came from the state of North Carolina.

The monsters were found at a place called "Tlanusi'yi" which means "the Leech Place." It is located where the Hiwassee and Valley Rivers meet in Cherokee County.

According to legend, the Cherokee people were warned by another tribe not to settle in the area because it was the home of a monster. These people told the Cherokee not to cross the river, for in it lived a monster leech that would eat them up. After settling there anyways, the Cherokee came to believe that the beast lived in an underwater cavern and that when it surfaced the water would boil and foam. The same thing would happen at a spot two miles away on the Nottely River. Because of that, the Cherokee believed an underground tunnel connected both spots where the leech was seen.

Though it spent most of its time under the water, the gigantic leech was often seen sunning itself on a rock ledge where the Hiwassee and Valley Rivers joined.

And it wasn't friendly either. One tale told of two men spotting the creature there one day, sunning itself as usual. They claimed that it had red and white stripes along its body. What happened next is so wild that it can only be folklore.

According to the story, the monster became so angry that the twisting of its tail created a wave that washed both men into the river.

The monster used the same trick on a young Cherokee man who tried to kill the beast, and he was washed into the river too.

Though the beast creating waves and whirlwinds with its tail is purely folkloric, is it possible that the legend was based on an actual creature? In the world of science, the largest recorded leech is the giant Amazon leech (*Haementeria ghilianii de Filippi*). The leeches grow to be eighteen inches long at the largest. Could one of these leeches have found their way into North America, where its size was greatly exaggerated?

Or, was the monster really as big as people said it was? If so, it could have been a giant prehistoric insect called the bristle worm. Like a leech, it lived underwater but measured about three feet long. It also had a nasty pair of jaws.

The Hiwassee Dam, which was constructed in the 1940s. Library of Congress Photo.

Today the giant leech monster is no longer seen, and the Hiwassee Dam was formed in 1940. Did it go extinct, or is it merely hiding out in its underwater cave?

A mud volcano located in Yellowstone National Park in 1912. Library of Congress Photo.

CHAPTER 17
MONSTER OF THE MUD VOLCANO

In Winder, Georgia is a boggy pond called the Nodoroc by the Creek Native American tribe. The word Nodoroc basically means "gateway to the underworld" in the Creek language. It was also said to be the home of a monster.

The Nodoroc is a natural formation known as a mud volcano. Just like the name implies, a mud volcano is a formation that spews hot mud rather than lava. Mud volcanos do this when super-heated water from under the ground shoots to the surface, causing an eruption of mud. As such, mud volcanos aren't really volcanoes in the true sense of the word, but you get the idea.

An early day pioneer, G.J.N. Wilson, described the Nodoroc in his book *The Early History of Jackson County*, published in 1914.

Wilson wrote that the Nodoroc looked like a lake made of "smoking, bubbling, bluish mud" which had the thickness of molasses. He said that the muddy waves had the appearance of a boiling pot of water, and that it was the most intense towards the center of the muddy pond. In the center was a funnel-shaped object, which was the "mud volcano" itself.

The funnel spewed super-heated steam that looked like smoke from a real volcano. Wilson also wrote of the area's horrible smell. Wilson said that "it produced such horrid feelings as to cause some people to faint and made others so sick that they had to be led away."

What made the location even spookier was its history. Because they believed it to be the gateway to the underworld, the Creek Tribe threw the bodies of their enemies into the pond.

And that's where the monster came in. The Creek Tribe called it the Wog. It looked like a gigantic dog; only it had a forked tongue like a snake. The head was like that of a bear's rather than a dog's, and its eyes glowed red. Oddly, its front legs were longer than its rear legs. It was said to be as big as a small horse.

In particular, the monster had a strange tail. It was long and bushy, but didn't taper to a point and was thick all the way through. It was pure white, in contrast with the Wog's black fur on the rest of its body. Some witnesses even thought the huge white tail was a flag when they saw it from a distance.

No matter what, the Wog's tail was always moving. The constant motion created a strange "whizzing sound" that could be heard more than "twenty-five or thirty steps" away. The Creek Tribe said that the Wog's tail had a special purpose. Whenever a body was dropped into the mud, it would leave a hole in the mud. The Wog would use its tail to smooth the hole over.

A grainy image of the Wog.

But, the Wog wasn't just seen by the Creek tribe. Settlers also saw it, or maybe I should say, heard it. You see, though the settlers believed in the Wog, none of them ever laid eyes on it. But they did hear it moving around outside their houses at night.

The Creek Tribe had kindly informed the settlers that the Wog would do them no harm so long as they didn't attack it. They told the settlers the best thing that they could do would be to run inside and keep a light burning in their homes if they heard it coming.

And true to the Creek Tribe's word, the Wog never harmed human nor animal. However, the Wog's appearance was so terrifying that some animals were later found dead of fright.

The Wog was first reported by settlers in the vicinity of the old Jug Tavern in 1809. When residents heard its strange, whirring tail, they would run inside. Sometimes the Wog would stick its forked tongue through the openings between the logs that made up the cabin walls! But, after it had done so, it would go away.

The most detailed encounter with the monster came from Alonzo Draper. Draper claimed that he was sitting outside one night with his daughter, Helen, and a visitor, Abe Trent, when, suddenly, their dog began to howl frightfully.

They peered into the distance and spied a pack of wolves. But soon it became evident that the wolves were not the cause of their dog's fright. The wolves were themselves frightened of something and began to run away. Draper then spied a dark object coming out of the woods. It appeared to be carrying a white flag. They watched as the "flag" began to wave and they heard a strange whirring noise. It wasn't a flag. It was the Wog's big white tail!

Draper recognized the creature first and cried out, "It's that infernal wog!" Draper grabbed his dog and took his daughter and their guest inside. They listened from inside the cabin to the strange noises the monster made. When it came near, it made a sound similar to the hissing of a goose.

The Wog stuck its forked tongue through an opening into the house. Draper grabbed his dog before it could bite the tongue and anger the monster. The Wog circled the house once more and then made a grunt similar to a wild hog's.

The family waited in the cabin for a long time before they heard a knock on their door. It was a neighbor there to tell them that he had seen the Wog going away and that they were now all safe.

That same night, the Wog also terrified a Native American camp at a place called Haitauthuga. It chased one of the tribe, a man named Siloquot, up a tree. But thankfully, the fearsome Wog could not climb because it had hooves rather than claws.

After the Civil War, the Wog wasn't seen again until many years later. In 2012, a soldier out for a run in the wilds near Fort Bennings, Georgia, saw it.

At first, he thought it was a hog sitting on the side of the road. He eventually began to notice that it had some notable differences from a hog, beginning with a long bushy tail and an exceptionally muscular chest. It sat up as high as a Great Dane, and its face was similar to a hog and a dog both. The creature looked at him and took a step forward. Afraid, the soldier ran away as fast as he could.

You might have noticed that the soldier said nothing about red eyes or a snake-like tongue. This is because the Wog was probably based upon a real animal, and its characteristics were greatly exaggerated over time.

Something similar to the Wog was killed in Montana in 1886. A rancher named Israel Hutchins shot the beast when it was chasing some geese on his ranch. Hutchins had the body taxidermied, and it still exists today. Or, in other words, there's proof that it was real. Scientists have wanted to run tests on the strange animal but have been denied access to it. As such, to this day, we still don't know what the creature from Montana is.

Like the Wog, it looks like a monstrous dog. Some have theorized that it's a Borophagus, a type of hyena-like dog from the Ice Age. But, until proper testing can be done, we'll never know for sure.

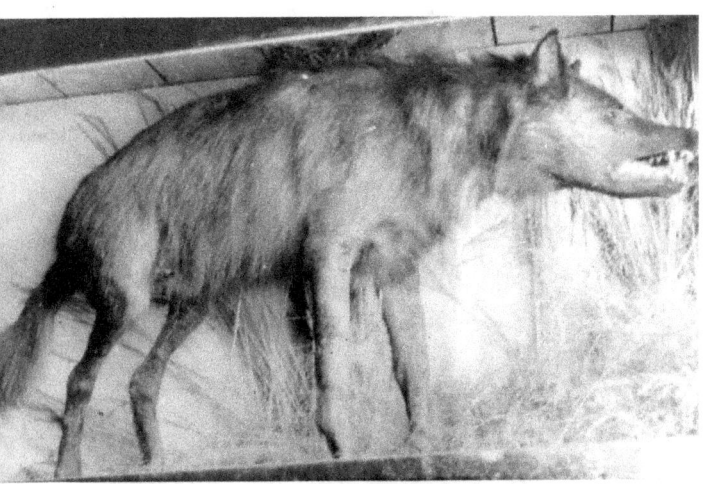

Mysterious dog-like animal killed in Montana in 1886.

CHAPTER 18
THE MISSISSIPI MONSTER

During the year 1877, the Mississippi River was terrorized by what appeared to be a sea serpent. But unlike most sea serpents, which looked like giant snakes, this one was quite odd looking.

The monster appeared in several articles and was said to have a snake-like body 30 feet long. Witnesses couldn't agree whether the head resembled a dog's or a seal's, but all agreed that it had a beak like a pelican's measuring five feet long. The monster's ears were also compared to a dog's. It was described as having scales that were either black or dark brown, depending on the witness. Its underside was dark blue like a catfish.

Along the neck it had a hairy mane like a horse or lion. The monster appeared to have four legs and two larger flippers. Its tail was fluked, like a whale's.

The monster was first seen in the late summer months, as men working along the river observed it moving through the water. Witnesses got a better look at it when it was discovered sunning itself like a snake on the beach of the river a few weeks later. A farmer named Jacob Erst was the first to see it. Erst ran to tell his neighbors that he had seen the monster. Erst returned to the spot with a large group of people, all of whom vouched for seeing the monster.

In hopes of capturing the creature, several men shot at it. Though the bullets hit the beast, they weren't enough to kill it. The monster let out an angry wail and scampered back into the river.

The monster wasn't seen again until the fall when it attacked a boat in the river in early October. The ship in question was a large tow-boat called the Bee Wing. The Bee Wing was towing several barges full of coal when the captain, John Carraway, heard a loud noise he thought came from another ship. But, to his horror, it was the Mississippi Monster, swimming behind his tow-barges!

The monster wasn't just following them; it was chasing them with harmful intent. It disappeared beneath the waters. Watching with great suspense, the captain wondered where it went. Then, suddenly, one of the barges of coal was bumped twenty feet into the air from something underneath it. Coal spilled into the water, and so too did a man on the barge, Henry Decker.

But, the monster didn't try to eat him. It was strangely focused on the coal barges, and attacked another. It began pecking and biting at the barge with its beak. For reasons unknown, the monster decided that its work was done. It stopped attacking the barges and quickly swam away from the boat to everyone's great relief.

Later, when inspecting one of the damaged barges, the captain found a splinter of the monster's beak stuck in the barge!

The Ohio River Monster as pictured in newspapers.

On January 12, 1878, another paper reported on how the monster had recently overturned a produce boat. Luckily, no one was eaten, though the witnesses certainly were scared.

This was the last major article on the Mississippi Monster, which seemed to disappear after that. Skeptics will say that newspaper writers simply got tired of making up stories starring the monster. However, in 1878 came several reports of a monster that looked just like the one from the Mississippi River seen in the Ohio River. Witnesses described it with all of the same traits: the beak, the hairy mane, and the slimy skin.

All things considered, it sounds as though the Mississippi Monster just decided to trade one river for another.

Tennessee Lizardman by Neil Riebe.

CHAPTER 19
THE TENNESSEE LIZARDMAN

Perhaps it's appropriate that since we began this book with the tale of a Lizard Man, that we shall also end it with one.

Sometime in the year 1878, a "wild man" was captured in the woods of Tennessee by a man named Dr. O.G. Broyler. Papers said that from a distance, the creature looked just like a man until one saw it close up. There, one could see that its skin was covered in scales like a reptile. The paper even reported that this Lizard Man would shed his skin once a season, just like a snake!

However, unlike the Alligator Man seen in South Carolina, this creature also had hair. The hair was just on its head, like a normal person. The hair was reddish in color and included a beard that was six inches long. But, the man had strange eyes that were about twice the size of a normal person's.

Other strange features unique to this "lizard man" were its webbed feet. He was also rather tall at six feet five inches.

According to Dr. Broyler, the Lizard Man wasn't a monster, because he was born to human parents. The parents had the last name of Creslin and lived in North Carolina. Their son was born sometime before the Civil War and, according to them, always had scaly skin like a reptile. The wild boy escaped his family at the age of five by running away and jumping into the water. He swam away never to be recaptured, though he was observed spending unusually long amounts of time under the water. There he would catch fish and eat them raw!

Dr. Broyler had wanted to catch the boy for some time but had to wait until after the Civil War was over. He didn't actually catch the Lizard Man until

MONSTERS OF THE OLD SOUTH

September 15, 1878. Dr. Broyler caught the Lizard Man's trail but had great difficulty capturing him. The Lizard Man, he said, was very fast and agile. It was all Dr. Broyler and his companions could do to keep up with the Lizard Man in hopes that he would eventually become tired.

At one point, the men tried to lasso him with a rope, but that didn't work. They finally captured him by setting a trap with a huge net. The Lizard Man was lured into it and trapped. But the battle wasn't over yet. The angry Lizard Man scratched and clawed at Dr. Broyler within the net and ended up wounding him badly.

But, Dr. Broyler recovered and managed to tame the Lizard Man to an extent. Though the man-thing eventually calmed down, after his capture, the Lizard Man was described as always itching to escape his captors. His muscles seemed to always be twitching, and he would eye doorways as though looking for an escape.

Articles on the man revealed that his skin needed to be kept wet, and that if his skin became too dry, he would become sickly and uneasy.

The Lizard Man didn't speak English but did occasionally seem to try and form words which no one could understand.

Dr. Broyler made a traveling show of the Lizard Man, taking him from town to town via wagon. An article makes mention of him being examined by several doctors who didn't know what to think of the strange man.

The newspaper article, published in the *Louisville Courier Journal* on October 24, 1878, concluded by writing, "The presence of the wild man in Louisville [Kentucky] has excited considerable attention among the doctors, and also a large crowd of curious persons who are anxious to see the wonderful creature. There will be only one exhibition in this city, which takes place at the Metropolitan Theatre Saturday evening."

Unfortunately, we don't know what happened to the mysterious Lizard Man after this, or if he was ever real at all.

About the Author

John LeMay was born and raised in Roswell, New Mexico, the town where aliens and a UFO allegedly crashed in 1947. He has written over twenty books on western history and folklore like this one. He is the co-author of the series *The Real Cowboys and Aliens* (about UFOs in the Old West) with Noe Torres and is also the author of the *Cowboys & Saurians* series, about dinosaur sightings from the Pioneer Period.

Also Available

www.ingramcontent.com/pod-product-compliance
Lightning Source LLC
Chambersburg PA
CBHW030255030426
42336CB00009B/383